P9-DEY-540

THE RED WOLF

THE RED WOLF

Alvin, Virginia, and Robert Silverstein

THE MILLBROOK PRESS, BROOKFIELD, CONNECTICUT

Library of Congress Cataloging-in-Publication Data
Silverstein, Alvin.
The red wolf / by Alvin, Virginia, and Robert Silverstein.
p.   cm.—(Endangered in America)
Includes bibliographical references (p.   ) and index.
Summary: By the mid-twentieth century red wolves had been
driven almost to extinction by the expanding human population.
This book describes these animals and the recovery program that
has begun to bring them back. It also examines the controversy
about the red wolf's relationship to the gray wolf and the coyote.
ISBN 1-56294-416-9 (lib. bdg.)
1. Red wolf—United States—Juvenile literature.   2. Endangered
species—United States—Juvenile literature.   3. Wildlife
reintroduction—United States—Juvenile literature.   [1. Red wolf.
2. Wolves.   3. Endangered species.   4. Wildlife reintroduction.]
I. Silverstein, Virginia B.   II. Silverstein, Robert A.   III. Title.
IV. Series: Silverstein, Alvin. Endangered in America.
QL737.C22S545   1994   333.95'9—dc20   93-42480   CIP   AC

Published by The Millbrook Press
2 Old New Milford Road, Brookfield, Connecticut 06804

Copyright © 1994 by Alvin, Virginia, and Robert Silverstein
All rights reserved
Printed in the United States of America
3   5   4

The authors would like to thank Robert R. Ream of the University of Montana School of Forestry for his careful reading of the manuscript and his helpful comments and suggestions.

Thanks also to Will Waddell of the Point Defiance Zoo and Aquarium in Tacoma, Washington; Michael Morse of the Alligator River National Wildlife Refuge; *Wolf!* magazine correspondent Lorraine Baretela; and all the others who generously shared information and insights about the red wolf and its recovery program.

Cover photograph courtesy of Mel Woods
Point Defiance Zoo and Aquarium

Photographs courtesy of Point Defiance Zoo and Aquarium:
pp. 8, 23 (Sue Behrns), 26, 28, 42 (all, Mel Woods);
Wild Canid Survival and Research Center: pp. 13 (Russ
Lampertz), 19, 32; U.S. Fish and Wildlife Service: pp.
15 (Steve Maslowski), 17 (Curtis Carley), 53; © Joni
Soffron: p. 21; © William Muñoz: pp. 24, 36, 44; USDA
Forest Service, Washington, D.C.: p. 33 (Barry Nehr);
Great Smoky Mountains National Park: pp. 39, 47; Thom
Lewis, U. S. Fish and Wildlife Service: p. 41.
Map by Joe Le Monnier

CONTENTS

The red wolf was hunted nearly to extinction.

WHO'S AFRAID OF THE BIG BAD WOLF?

We think of dogs as loyal, loving friends. But wolves, close relatives of domestic dogs, are usually seen as bloodthirsty killers. As children, we learn that the Big Bad Wolf huffed and puffed and blew down the homes of two of the three little pigs, and the Wicked Wolf gobbled up Little Red Riding Hood's grandmother. Evil werewolves, like vampires, are frequent villains in scary horror stories. And we should "never cry wolf!" or we'll be sorry. These are views of wolves that people have had for many generations. European settlers brought these ideas with them when they came to America.

Native Americans knew that all creatures, even wolves, played an important role in the balance of nature. But when European settlers came to America, they had a different way of looking at things. They changed the land to suit their plans. Some animals, such as wolves, did not fit into those plans.

There were plenty of opportunities for conflict. Wolves competed with human hunters for elk and deer. As forests were cleared and marshes drained to make room for farms and villages, there was less food for the wolves to hunt. So they sometimes killed sheep and cattle. Coyotes, which prefer open, drier areas, moved in from the north and west. They put further pressure on the wolves by competing for the remaining prey.

The settlers had brought their fear and hatred of wolves with them, too, and thought these native predators were a threat to their own lives. They went after the wolves with guns, traps, and poison.

Bounties have been offered for killing wolves in almost every state going back to 1630 in the Massachusetts Bay Colony. Between 1600 and 1950, close to two million wolves were killed in America. Nearly all the wolves in most of the United States were killed. In fact, one type of wolf, the red wolf, had nearly become extinct by the 1970s. Fortunately, the government started a program to save the red wolf. Scientists took the few remaining red wolves into captivity and helped them to breed. Today there are more than 200 red wolves, and some of them have been returned to the wild.

Environmental organizations helped to set aside large tracts of protected land where red wolves can be reintroduced into the wild. But there are many obstacles to overcome before scientists can return enough of these animals to the wild for them to survive on their own. The biggest obstacle is the attitude about wolves that nearly made them extinct in the first place.

WOLVES AREN'T REALLY "BAD GUYS"

Wolves don't deserve their fearsome reputation. Actually, they have many traits that people admire. They mate for life. They live in family groups of parents, children, and close relatives. The family members work together as a team to raise the pups, find food, and defend each other against enemies.

Wolves are not really a threat to people, either. No healthy wolf of any kind has ever attacked a person in the United States. (Rabid wolves, just like any animal with rabies, may attack humans.) Wolves are actually afraid of people, and the biologists who study them have found it very difficult to get close enough to observe them. Even wolves raised in captivity are never totally comfortable around people.

Wolves haven't always been hated. In Rudyard Kipling's *Jungle Book* tales, Mowgli, the jungle boy, was raised by a loving family of wolves. In Roman mythology, a female wolf nursed Romulus and Remus, the twins who founded Rome. Native American warriors and ancient European kings proudly included the word "wolf" in their names to show that they were brave and strong.

WORKING TOWARD A NEW BEGINNING

People nearly caused the red wolf to become extinct. Now people are helping to save it and return it to the wild. "When nature is left to its own devices, extinction is a natural and even vital process. But the red wolf was not on its way to extinction until people intervened. Now we've intervened again—this time on its behalf," said Warren Parker, the coordinator of a federal plan to save the red wolf.[1]

While scientists work to save the red wolves, others are working hard to educate the public, so people will understand that wolves deserve a place in our world, too.

THE RED WOLF

Wolves are the largest wild members of the dog family. They are related to coyotes, foxes, jackals, dingoes, and domestic dogs. (The members of the dog family are called canids, from *Canis*, their scientific name.) Wolves are actually the ancestors of all the many different kinds of domestic dogs, from tiny Chihuahuas to Great Danes and German shepherds. Prehistoric people domesticated wolves and found that they were intelligent and loyal companions. Over thousands of years the domesticated wolves evolved into the many breeds of dogs we have today.

THE TWO KINDS OF WOLVES

Scientists believe there are two kinds, or species, of wolves: gray wolves and red wolves. (Their scientific names are *Canis lupus* and *Canis rufus*.) Since prehistoric times, gray wolves have lived all across the Northern Hemisphere—in North America, Europe, and Asia.

Gray wolves are not necessarily gray. Their fur may range from white to black, and most have coats of many shades, including gray, brown, tan, and black. Timber wolves, arctic wolves, buffalo wolves, tundra wolves,

This Mexican wolf is one of several types of gray wolves.

and Mexican wolves are all gray wolves. At least 32 different subspecies of gray wolves have been identified, but some of them have become extinct. Each subspecies is a little different because each evolved to live in a different habitat.

Red wolves were first described by the noted naturalist William Bartram in 1791. Found only in the southern United States, they were first called red wolves in 1851. Today some scientists are not so sure that the

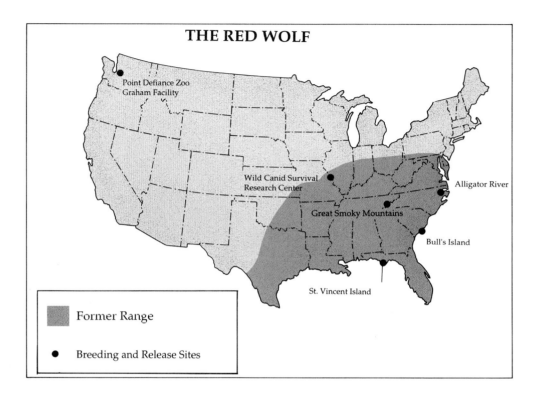

THE RED WOLF

Point Defiance Zoo
Graham Facility

Wild Canid Survival
Research Center

Alligator River

Great Smoky Mountains

Bull's Island

St. Vincent Island

Former Range

Breeding and Release Sites

red wolves are actually a separate species. Some believe the red wolf is a subspecies of the gray wolf. Others think the red wolf is a hybrid of the gray wolf and its close relative, the coyote.

Before European settlers came to America, red wolves lived in dense coastal thickets, central plains, southern swamps, and coastal marshes from the coasts of Georgia and Florida west to central Texas. There may have been three subspecies of red wolves at one time, in different areas of the southern United States. The eastern and western species are now extinct. Scientists were able to rescue only the central subspecies.

Red wolves are smaller than gray wolves and bigger than coyotes. They weigh between 40 and 70 pounds (18 and 32 kilograms). Like the

A smaller build and bigger ears are among the features that make the red wolf different from gray wolves.

gray wolf, the name "red wolf" is also misleading. Their coats are typically tan or cinnamon-brown, streaked with black. Some coats have a gold or reddish tint. They can also be all gray, black, or yellowish.

Red wolves have brownish-yellow eyes. Their ears are long and shaped like those of a German shepherd, much larger than the ears of gray wolves. That is a reflection of the climate of the wolves' homes; gray wolves usually live in colder climates, where their short ears have less chance of becoming frostbitten.

WOLVES ARE WELL-DESIGNED HUNTERS

Wolves are nocturnal animals. That means they are active and hunt at night. They are *carnivores*, or meat-eaters. They have sharp canine teeth (fangs) up to 2 inches (5 centimeters) long, which they use to kill weaker animals. Other teeth grind bones and rip off meat. These days many people are cutting down on the amount of meat they eat because the fat and cholesterol that meat contains can lead to heart disease. But carnivores' bodies are equipped to handle an all-meat diet with no harmful effects.

There is a good reason why people use the expression "hungry as a wolf" to mean that a person is very hungry. Wolves gulp down big chunks of meat. A red wolf can "wolf down" 15 pounds (6.8 kilograms) of meat in one meal, and a gray wolf may eat even more! Their stomachs stretch to hold all this food. Wolves stuff themselves this way because they may not have a chance to eat regularly. They may go as long as two weeks between meals.

A wolf's body is well designed to hunt animals that may even be larger than it is. Wolves have strong, agile bodies. A dog the same size is only one third as strong as a wolf. Wolves have much longer legs and bigger feet than most domestic dogs. This helps them walk through swampy marshes with tall grass. A red wolf can run at speeds of up to about 30 miles (48 kilometers) per hour and can jump 6 to 7 feet (1.8 to 2 meters) straight up in the air with ease. (Captive red wolves have jumped out of pens with a 9-foot fence.)

A red wolf's long legs helps it run fast, even over wet ground.

Wolves can hear softer and higher pitched sounds than we can hear. Their sense of smell is 100 times better than ours; a wolf can pick up the scent of prey up to 1½ miles (2.4 kilometers) away.

Gray wolves can prey on large animals such as elk and buffalo. Red wolves prefer smaller animals such as raccoons, rabbits, squirrels, muskrats, rats, fish, and even insects and plant material. But they may also hunt small deer or eat deer killed by cars on roads and highways. Food that is not eaten right away may be buried or hidden in a hollow log.

The Balance of Nature

ONE OF the reasons people are afraid of wolves is that wolves prey on other animals. But this is just the way nature works. All living things are part of a balance in nature.

A particular habitat where animals live can be thought of as an *ecosystem*. Every plant and animal in an ecosystem has its own place, and other living things are dependent on it. Plants get their food from the soil, water, air, and the sun. Some animals eat plants. These plant-eating animals are *prey* for meat-eating animals. Meat-eating animals that hunt for prey are called *predators*.

If there are not enough predators in an ecosystem, plant-eating animals will reproduce too quickly, causing a population explosion. The increased number of prey animals may not be able to find enough plant food to survive. As they die of starvation, predators have trouble finding enough food, too. Eventually the ecosystem may fall apart as all the plants are eaten, and the animals begin to die in great numbers.

Wolves were once the main predators in North America, helping to keep the numbers of animals such as rabbits and deer in balance.

A gray wolf establishes dominance with a show of aggression.

A TYPICAL WOLF FAMILY

Wolves are sociable animals and live in family units, called packs. A gray wolf pack, which may include up to ten animals, is led by the largest and strongest male. He and his mate are called the alpha pair, and they are dominant over all the other members of the pack. The pack includes the children of the alpha pair and other related adults. Each wolf has a rank in the pack, and a wolf is dominant over the wolves that are lower in rank.

Scientists are just beginning to learn how red wolves behave in the wild. There are old reports of packs of wolves in the South, but by the time people really began to study red wolves there were very few of them left. Some red wolves hunt alone, or in small groups of two or three. But some of the red wolves now living wild in protected areas have formed small packs. After the first season, some of the young wolves leave their parents to go off on their own, but some young adults may remain with the family group. Both parents care for the young pups, and the young adults may help out by "baby-sitting."

The alpha pair are the only wolves in the pack that breed. They are always the first ones to eat. Lower-ranked wolves eat when those higher in rank are finished. In all activities, the pack takes its cues from the alpha pair. Rank may change over the years, as the wolves get older and their hunting skills and physical strength change.

Packs wander over great distances to find food to eat. This range of 30 to 250 square miles (about 80 to 650 square kilometers) or more is their territory, and other wolf packs are not welcome on it. The wolves carefully mark their territory with urine and feces to warn other packs not to trespass.

HOWLING AT THE MOON

Wolves have very sophisticated ways of communicating with each other. They can communicate well with body language. When wolves interact, the alpha male and female stand tall, hold their tails high, and prick up their ears. The lower-ranked wolves crouch down, flatten their ears, and lower their tails whenever the pack leaders approach them. Raising the ears, the tail, and the fur on the wolf's mane is a threat. When threatened, a low-ranking wolf will roll onto its back, or tuck its tail between its legs. A male may flatten his ears to show his mate he is in a romantic mood.

Wolves also whimper, bark, growl, whine, yelp, snarl, and howl to get their messages across. If a stranger intrudes on the pack's territory, barking is a warning or threat. Growling is also a threat or a sign of anger. To call or calm their pups, adult wolves whimper, whine, or make soft, mouselike squeaks.

Howling is, of course, their best-known way of communicating. When wolves separate, they howl back and forth to keep in touch with each other. The wolf pack howl together as a social ritual. They may howl before or after a hunt, or when they return to the den or resting site. Each

Howling is an important social ritual for wolf packs.

wolf's voice is different, with almost musical ranges. They close their eyes and howl in off-key chords, sounding almost like an eerie choir. The sound can be heard up to 4 miles (6.4 kilometers) away.

LIFE CYCLE OF A WOLF

Red wolves breed in February or March of their second or third year. The young develop inside their mother's body for 63 days and are born sometime between late April and early June. Three to four weeks before the pups are born, the female wolf begins to dig out a den. She may spend several days looking for just the right spot. The den may be in a hollow log or along the banks of a canal or a ditch. Sometimes the wolf enlarges a woodchuck burrow or a fox den. The male may help her. First a 6- to 14-foot (about 2- to 4-meter) tunnel is dug. The tunnel slopes upward so that rain cannot get in, and it is small enough to prevent large animals from crawling inside. At the end of the tunnel the female digs out one or two rooms, high enough for her to stand up in. The pups are born shortly after the tunnel is finished.

Two to six pups are born 10 to 60 minutes apart. The pups each weigh about a pound (0.5 kilogram) at birth. They are covered with dark fur and have large, round heads with pug noses. Like domestic puppies, red wolf pups are helpless at first, and their eyes do not open until two weeks after birth. Like all mammals, they drink milk from their mother. For the first ten to twelve days, all they do is drink milk and sleep. The mother leaves the den only to drink. The male brings her food.

A few days after wolf pups open their eyes, they crawl out of the den for the first time. When they are three weeks old, the pups can start eating solid food. The adults may have traveled far to find food, so they store it in

A female red wolf and her pups.

special compartments in their stomachs. They spit up partly digested food when the pups lick their jaws. Fresh prey is brought to the den when the pups are eight weeks old and ready to be weaned.

Wolf pups play outside the den entrance as they grow. Their play resembles many games that human children play—tug-of-war, tag, and keep away. They also wrestle and play quite a bit more roughly than children are allowed to. But their wrestling and romping together is more than just play. They are strengthening their muscles to prepare for hunting. Pouncing on twigs and on each other teaches them how to stalk and sneak up on prey. The pups are also establishing their rank in the pack. Usually the stronger pup wins a wrestling match, and the loser rolls over on its back to give up. Pack members quickly learn to "follow the leader."

When the pups are about three or four months old, they are able to take care of themselves. But they usually remain with their parents and hunt in small packs for another year or two. They will not be fully mature until they are about two years old.

Red wolf pups are ready to crawl out of the den a few days after their eyes open.

EXTINCT IN THE WILD

Red wolves were once found throughout the southeastern United States, as far north as Pennsylvania and as far west as central Texas. This is the original range of the eastern forests up to the point where the western grasslands take over. In 1600 there were probably about 100,000 red wolves, but by the 1960s so many had been killed that scientists began to be concerned about the fate of the red wolf.

DECLINE OF THE RED WOLF

In 1962, biologist Howard McCarley published a study warning that red wolves were interbreeding with coyotes. When the forests and marshes where red wolves lived were cleared for farming and herding livestock, coyotes quickly moved into these open lands. Red wolf numbers had decreased so much that some of them could not find mates and mated instead with coyotes. Their hybrid offspring looked like wolves, but for fifteen years McCarley had noticed that the "red wolves" of the South seemed to be getting smaller. "Everybody called them wolves. But they just didn't look like wolves to me," he says.[2] McCarley examined wolf

As the forests and marshes where they lived were taken over by people, the number of red wolves decreased.

skulls collected throughout the South and noticed that they were smaller than the skulls of red wolves that had been collected in the same areas in the 1920s and 1930s.

When his study was published, government officials requested that predator-control officers bring in the skulls of all wolflike animals they killed. But there was no attempt to protect the few remaining red wolves. Many biologists began to search for red wolves and found that they had nearly disappeared from many areas where it had been thought they were still plentiful. In the mid-1960s, the red wolf was added to the federal list of endangered species, but still the government continued to fund predator-control programs that included shooting and poisoning red wolves in the last remaining places where they were found.

No detailed studies were made of the red wolf until the late 1960s. But by then the small number of wolves that were left were crowded into small areas of coastal Texas and Louisiana. They were forced to live in low, wet marshes, among ranches, oil fields, and oil refineries.

HELP FOR AN ENDANGERED ANIMAL

In 1968, the Fish and Wildlife Service, the government agency that manages wildlife, assigned a biologist to investigate reports of wolves on ranchers' properties. Instead of being killed, the wolves were to be captured. In 1969, Texan Glynn Riley took over this position. Riley found the red wolves were in very bad health. Mange, a skin ailment caused by tiny mites, destroyed their fur and left patches of bare skin. Hookworm parasites killed many red wolf puppies; heartworms weakened and eventually killed many adults. "They were skinny and rat-tailed. If one of them lived five years, he was doing good, the habitat was so bad," Riley says.[3]

Local bounties were no longer paid for bringing in dead wolves, and Riley convinced ranchers not to shoot the wolves but to let him trap them. Riley relocated the wolves to places such as a nearby wildlife refuge. Some were sent to Minnesota, where a researcher was conducting tests to determine the genetic makeup of wolves and coyotes. But it got harder to find places that would take them. When Riley caught what looked like a pure red wolf, he took it to a nearby veterinarian, who would keep the wolf for a while. The veterinarian often treated Riley's sick and injured wolves without charge. When the ranchers' tempers had cooled down, Riley and his veterinarian friend would quietly release the wolf somewhere away from the ranch where it had been causing trouble.

Workers at the Point Defiance Zoo restrain a pair of captive red wolves. The Tacoma, Washington, zoo set up the first red wolf captive-breeding program.

Meanwhile, some conservationists had been talking about breeding the red wolf in captivity. In 1970, the board of directors at Point Defiance Zoo and Aquarium in Tacoma, Washington, had three pens built for red wolves. Thirteen wolves were shipped to Tacoma between 1970 and 1972, but few survived.

When Riley began tracking red wolves, there were about 100 of them on the Texas coast, but that number was rapidly decreasing and the number of hybrids was increasing. Riley knew that relocating the wolves would not save them from extinction. But the government would not provide any additional funds to help save the red wolf. (The federal agency in charge of endangered species at the time was the same agency that had paid trappers to kill the red wolf over most of its range.)

In 1973 the Endangered Species Act was passed. This major law provided protection for animals and plants in danger of becoming extinct. Now the red wolf recovery was finally given a larger budget. Curtis Carley came to Texas to head an expanded Red Wolf Recovery Program. The plan was to collect red wolves for a breeding program at the Point Defiance Zoo and to make sure that a healthy number of red wolves survived in the wild.

The biologists were to clear a 15-mile-wide (24-kilometer-wide) buffer zone around the last remaining red wolf territory Only red wolves would be allowed; hybrids and coyotes had to be removed. But by 1974 it became apparent that wolf-coyote hybrids had already spread through the whole Texas coast area.

REMOVING THE RED WOLF FROM THE WILD

The scientists were worried that even if the remaining red wolves were able to survive in the wild, eventually there would not be any pure red wolves left, only hybrids. In 1975, it was decided that all the remaining purebred red wolves would be taken into captivity to keep the species alive. But how could they determine which wolves were red wolves and which were hybrids? They couldn't just go by appearance because some of the hybrids looked like red wolves.

The biologists could have determined which animals were pure red wolves and which had some coyote genes by breeding them. If the parents were hybrids, some of the pups would show coyote traits. But there wasn't enough room or time to breed all the animals in order to test them, so the biologists had to rely on other clues. They looked at the general body proportions, weight, and whether the animal howled like a wolf. Skull measurements became an important tool. X rays were taken to compare the skull size and shape with a standard red wolf skull.

Over a number of years the U.S. Fish and Wildlife Service checked 400 wild canids from the Sabine River basin. Most of the wolves examined were actually red wolf/coyote hybrids. Only 40 were believed to be pure red wolves. They were shipped to the Point Defiance Zoo, which in 1973 had been chosen by the Fish and Wildlife Service as the official government breeding center for red wolves.

The zoo had limited space, but a nearby mink farmer, Dale Pedersen, was working with the zoo biologists. He had already set up two pens on his farm in Graham, Washington, and had been housing red wolves at his own expense for a year by the time the project officially got under way. "I decided that as long as I was going to breed animals, I may as well breed some for a good cause," he says.[4]

While the Wolf's Away . . .

SCIENTISTS know that when an animal becomes extinct in the wild, a related species will move in to take its place in its geographic and biological niche. Sure enough, five years after the last red wolf was taken from the wild and shipped to the Point Defiance Zoo breeding program, coyotes had completely taken over the Sabine River valley.

The 40 wolves underwent many blood tests. The animals were bred with each other to see if coyotelike pups were born. Eventually only 17 of the wolves were found to be pure enough, with at least 95 percent red wolf genes.

THE SUCCESS OF BREEDING PROGRAMS

"We were not even sure," recalls Curtis Carley, "when the decision was made to take every wolf out of the wild, that we would be able to breed them well in captivity."[5] The breeding project started by trial and error, as the zoo biologists improvised equipment and worked out techniques for handling the wolves and treating their ailments with the least possible stress. Some of the wolves were too old or sick to survive. But others thrived, and their fur thickened and grew darker.

The first pair of red wolves that arrived at the mink ranch bred and produced a litter in the spring of 1974. But during the following years the breeding program began to look like a disastrous failure. Not one pair of captive red wolves was able to raise any healthy pups in 1975 or 1976.

Finally, in 1977, mated pairs produced several red wolf litters at the breeding facility. By 1980, the number of red wolves in captivity had increased to more than 50—but wildlife biologists in the field reported that no more wild red wolves could be found. That year the red wolf was officially declared extinct in the wild.

The captive breeding program was doing well. But 50 animals were too few to try to rebuild a whole species. An epidemic at the breeding center, for example, could have wiped them all out. To reduce the risk, some of the Point Defiance animals were sent to breeding centers in other parts of the country.

Enclosures at the Wild Canid Survival and Research Center.

The Wolf Sanctuary

THE Wild Canid Survival and Research Center, also called the Wolf Sanctuary, was founded in 1971 by the late Marlin Perkins, host of the popular TV wildlife show *Wild Kingdom*, and his wife, Carol, who wanted people to understand that wolves are an important part of nature. The Wolf Sanctuary, located near Eureka, Missouri, works with the U.S. Fish and Wildlife Service and zoos to provide space, funds, and staff to care for and breed red wolves and other rare wolves, as well as providing tours and educating the public about wolves.

A red wolf at a research center near St. Louis, Missouri. To guarantee the survival of the species, breeding programs were started at several sites.

In 1980, a red wolf breeding program was set up at the Audubon Zoological Park in New Orleans, Louisiana. The next year the Wild Canid Survival & Research Center in Eureka, Missouri, became the second breeding site outside of Tacoma. In 1984, the red wolf was added to the Species Survival Program set up by the American Association of Zoological Parks & Aquariums. This program is dedicated to preserving the original genetic uniqueness of an animal population through careful management.

Since then at least 20 zoos and other facilities have taken part in red wolf recovery, although the Point Defiance Zoo program has remained the core of the program. (By the early 1990s, nearly one-third of the total population of red wolves could still be found there.)

RETURN TO THE WILD

It was always the goal of the recovery program to return red wolves to their natural habitat as soon as possible. In 1976, a pair of wild red wolves, Buddy and Margie, were freed experimentally on 5,000-acre (2,000-hectare) Bulls Island off the coast of South Carolina. After only a week, though, Margie was frightened by a German shepherd on a nearby island and fled back to the mainland, crossing 3 miles (almost 5 kilometers) of salt marsh before she was recaptured. Analyzing the experiment afterward, the researchers decided that the wolves had not had a long enough time to get used to their new surroundings before they were released.

In 1978, the experiment was tried again with another pair, John and Judy. The wolves were kept in a pen on the island for six months before being released. This time the experiment was a success. The scientists were able to track the wolves' activities using radio transmitters, and John and Judy were recaptured the following year, when the experiment was over. The scientists began to look for permanent release sites.

The goal of the Red Wolf Recovery Plan is to have about 225 red wolves in the wild. But there were many obstacles to overcome before any red wolves could be released. First, the right habitat had to be found. Each wolf pair roams over large areas that cannot overlap with the territory of other wolf pairs. To establish big enough populations of red wolves, huge

In a holding pen. a red wolf family awaits release on Bull's Island. South Carolina.

tracts of land are needed. The areas must be isolated from people and livestock, and yet accessible enough for the wildlife biologists to study and protect the wolves. The largest obstacle, however, is public opinion. People are still afraid of wolves, and this would be the first large predator that was ever reintroduced into the wild in all the world.

In the early 1980s, the Fish and Wildlife Service proposed reintroducing captive-born red wolves into a 170,000-acre (68,800-hectare) federal recreational area called Land Between the Lakes in Kentucky and Tennessee. The decision was announced at a press conference. But everyone was against it. Farmers and hunters were angry and fearful. Even wildlife groups such as Defenders of Wildlife were against the plan because they thought there were too many hunters and coyotes in the area. The plan was canceled, but it taught the red wolf recovery team an important lesson: The public must become involved early in any release program.

Warren Parker, coordinator of the Wildlife Service's red wolf program, read that the conservation group Nature Conservancy had arranged for the Prudential Insurance Company to donate more than 100,000 acres (40,470 hectares) of forest and coastal marsh in North Carolina to be included in the national refuge system in 1984. He began studying the area as a possible release site.

The new Alligator River National Wildlife Refuge that was set up near the coast of North Carolina wasn't an ideal spot. Jets frequently flew over the swampy woods to test lasers and bombs on a nearby testing range. The local people told the biologists that the Alligator River peninsula was full of ticks, deer flies, and chiggers, and hookworm was common among the few foxes that lived there.

Could red wolves survive there? Conservationists designing recovery programs for predators have to be practical. The programs must be easy for people to adjust to, so that the animals can survive without interfering or conflicting with people. The land for the new refuge had been donated partly because it was not suitable for development. Conditions there were not ideal, but were better than the miserable conditions in the Sabine River valley, where the wolves had been barely clinging to existence. And there weren't any coyotes at the Alligator River site.

THE RED WOLF RETURNS TO THE WILD

The U.S. Fish and Wildlife Service began a year-long campaign to educate the public about the red wolf, enlisting the help of local conservation groups. Public meetings were held to explain the project and clear up misconceptions about wolves. Many people were reassured when they learned about the "capture collar" each wolf would wear. This device contains a radio transmitter to track the wolves and tranquilizer darts that can be activated by remote control to knock out a wolf so that it can be recaptured before it gets into trouble.

Four pairs of red wolves were shipped to Alligator River National Wildlife Refuge in November 1986 for the first release program in the nation. (Seven came from the Point Defiance Zoo, and one from the Wolf Sanctuary.)

Scientists were still not sure whether the wolves, which had lived in captivity for several generations, would be able to adjust to the wild. The eight wolves were placed in acclimation pens to get used to the area. They remained there for six months. At first they were fed dog food, then dead animals. Finally live animals were released in the pens. "When we put live raccoons in the pens, the wolves immediately knew what they had to do. We knew they were ready to be released. Even after three or four generations in captivity, they were fully capable of being placed back in the wild and surviving," Parker says.[6]

A red wolf wears a "capture collar" that contains
a radio transmitter and tranquilizer darts.

In September 1987, after nearly two decades of planning, the pen doors were opened and, eventually, the wolves wandered off.

REINTRODUCTION A SUCCESS

The reintroduction program was launched, but there were many problems and setbacks along the way. A few weeks after being released, one of the male wolves had to be recaptured because he had made his way to a nearby town and was eating out of dog dishes. He and his mate were relocated. But two weeks later the female died from an infection.

Another male was recaptured when his collar malfunctioned. He had been in a fight with another wolf and was badly wounded. While he was recovering under supervision, his mate wandered off the refuge twice, and was recaptured. But she died after getting into a territorial fight with another wolf.

The female from the Wolf Sanctuary was left to raise her pup alone when her mate was killed on the highway. Another male successfully raised a pup after his mate died from an infection.

Of the first twelve wolves released, two were hit by cars as they searched for food. One wolf choked while eating a raccoon. One wolf was killed in a fight with another wolf. And two wolves died from diseases.

Even with these setbacks, the reintroduction of red wolves at the Alligator River National Wildlife Refuge was hailed as a success. About half of the wolves have survived after release. The survival rate of pups born in the program is typical of that in the wild, and the surviving pups are healthy and vigorous.

In April 1988, the first litter of pups was born in the wild at the Alligator River National Wildlife Refuge. By the end of 1992, the rein-troduction program had involved 79 red wolves and produced at least 22 wild-born wolves. Some of the animals in the program were returned to captivity, but by the fall of 1993 at least 40 wolves were roaming free in eastern North Carolina, and half had been born in the wild.

CHANGING GOALS

As biologists gained experience in the reintroduction program, they began to realize that the refuge would not be able to support as many red wolves as they had originally hoped. The ideal goal of establishing a completely wild red wolf population, which would thrive without any help from humans, was not realistic either—at least, not yet.

Gradually the goals of the program shifted, from the establishment of a completely wild population to something more practical. Wildlife biologists would have to give the wolves supplements of food and heartworm medicine. Sick or injured animals might have to be rescued and given medical treatment before being released again. And to keep the local red wolf population from becoming too inbred, some wolves would have to be taken out of the refuge and relocated to other breeding colonies, and replaced with new wolves carrying different combinations of genes.

Researchers draw blood from a red wolf. Even after release, biologists will monitor the animals' health.

A Captive-Breeding First

THREE red wolf pups born at the breeding facility in Graham, Washington, in May 1992, were the first reported litter of wild canids ever born to a mother who was artificially inseminated. (That is, researchers placed a sample of semen, the fluid containing the sex cells, or sperm, from a male red wolf, into the female's body. Just as in a normal mating, the sperm then combined with the female's egg cells to start the lives of the pups.) Researchers hope to maintain the genetic diversity of the red wolf population by freezing and storing semen. By artificial insemination, the genes of the sperm-donor fathers can be passed on to future generations of pups long after the fathers have died.

The birth of these three pups in 1992 was an important first for the captive-breeding program.

(When any animal or human population breeds only with close relatives for a long time, there is a danger that hereditary diseases and weaknesses might become common and threaten the group's survival. Genetic diversity—a varied mixture of hereditary factors—can help to keep a species healthy and strong.) Eventually, the Alligator River refuge came to be seen as a sort of temporary homeland, where captive-born red wolves could learn to live and breed in the wild.

ISLAND BREEDING

The success at Alligator River led to the island breeding project. Breeding pairs of red wolves are released on islands to reproduce and raise their pups in the wild. Then they are caught to be released at other sites.

In 1987 a pair of wolves was shipped to Bulls Island, where the first experimental release had taken place, to establish the first wild breeding program on an island.

Three pups were born on the island in 1988, but in September 1989 Hurricane Hugo hit the coast of South Carolina, submerging the island under 19 feet (5.8 meters) of water. Miraculously, four days later when Warren Parker and his staff were able to get to the island, they found the three pups and two adults in the usual place. The scientists were not sure how the wolves had survived, but guessed that they crawled onto floating trees. However, two weeks later the adult male died from injuries suffered during the hurricane.

Horn Island, a 14-mile-long (23-kilometer-long) island off the coast of Mississippi, was chosen as another breeding site. A four-year-old male from Audubon Zoo and a five-year-old female from Point Defiance Zoo were placed in an acclimation pen. The female became pregnant and had

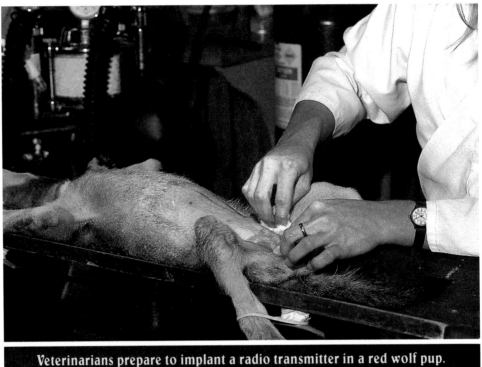

Veterinarians prepare to implant a radio transmitter in a red wolf pup. The transmitter will allow researchers to track the wolf after it is released.

seven pups (a normal litter is three to four pups) in May 1989. The animals were fitted with radio transmitters so scientists could keep track of them as they roamed the island.

Fish and Wildlife Service biologists continued to provide food for the wolves for three weeks, but the animals soon showed that they did not need any supplements. The adults had been fed dried dog food all their lives, but they quickly learned how to hunt and provide food for their young in the strange surroundings.

When the pups were only four months old, just half grown, their mother died of pancreatic cancer. (This is extremely rare in canids. Some biologists are worried that generations of captivity may have lowered the disease-fighting abilities of red wolves.) But the male raised the pups himself. Soon some of the pups were going out on their own, hunting and then meeting up with their father later. Usually three or four pups stayed with the small pack.

The wolves remained on the small island for a year and a half, and although 30,000 to 40,000 visitors came there each year, none ever spotted one. This has helped convince scientists and the public that severe restrictions on people's use of the land are not necessary for the wolves to survive. (At the Alligator River refuge, the people who lived near the area were allowed to continue hunting with dogs and trapping in the swamps, without conflict or harm to the released red wolves. In fact, many of the local people grew so fond of the wolves that the nearby town of Manteo adopted the red wolf as its symbol.)

In 1990, red wolves were released on Saint Vincent's Island in Florida and Durante Island in North Carolina.

THE GREAT SMOKY MOUNTAINS

The Alligator River National Wildlife Refuge is not big enough to be the home for very many wolves, so conservationists are looking for other sites. Wildlife experts believe the 500,000-acre (more than 200,000-hectare) Great Smoky Mountains National Park in Tennessee and North Carolina may be the only area in the Southeast large enough and wild enough for a breeding population of red wolves.

Red wolves had not lived in the Great Smoky Mountains since 1905! The long-range goal is for a steady population of between 50 and 75 red wolves in the park. But before a major program could begin, scientists had to make sure that the Smokies would be a suitable habitat for permanent reintroduction of red wolves.

Two adult wolves were brought from St. Vincent's Island National Wildlife Refuge in Florida to the Great Smoky Mountains National Park early in 1991. They stayed in an acclimation pen at first, and in April five pups were born there. In November 1991, the two adults and two of the seven-month-old pups were released at the park. The other three pups were taken to the Alligator River National Wildlife Refuge. Another pair was released at another site in the park in 1992.

Not Wild Enough Yet

ONE OF the first wolves introduced at the Great Smoky project helped himself to three turkeys from a nearby farm. Even when the farmer came out and chased him, the wolf calmly sat down at the edge of the woods to eat his turkey dinner. (When the farmer was offered a payment for his lost stock, he turned it down.)

Chris Lucash, the head of the project, had to recapture the wolf and remove him from the experiment. "He had spent too much of his life in captivity," Lucash says. "He was too comfortable with people." The biologists had expected this kind of problem. "We can't get around that until we get pups born and raised in the open forest," says Lucash. "We're just going to have to work real hard to get the animals through this transition until they start reproducing as real wild animals."[7]

A red wolf awaits release in Great Smoky Mountains National Park.

Biologists from the U.S. Fish and Wildlife Service, the park, and the University of Tennessee radio-tracked the wolves around the clock to determine their home range, diet, and relationships to humans, livestock, and coyotes. By the spring of 1993 there were four adult pairs at Great Smoky Mountains National Park. Two gave birth to litters in April 1993— the first red wolves born wild in the Great Smoky Mountains in nearly a century! (Two litters of red wolf pups had already been born in the Great Smokies park while their parents were still in acclimation pens.)

The reintroduction is already having some positive side effects, too. The park is plagued by wild boars, which were introduced into the park in this century. Park rangers had hoped the wolves would help control the population, as the boars have no natural predators there. And shortly after the reintroduced wolves began to hunt in their new territory, the project biologists were pleasantly surprised one day to find them standing in a creek with a freshly killed 70-pound (32-kilogram) wild pig.

WOLVES WILL BE WOLVES

When wolves stray from the protected parks, they are recaptured and then rereleased. If a wolf continually strays, it is returned to one of the breeding programs.

From the beginning of the recovery program, scientists knew that, wolves being wolves, the red wolves released into the wild might wander onto nearby private land and kill a farmer's chickens or calves. Even though red wolves are "threatened" animals, wolves released in the Smokies are listed as "experimental-nonessential," so that property owners can protect their livestock. (To help the public better accept the reintroduction of species such as red wolves into the wild, Congress amended the Endangered Species Act in 1982 to list reintroduced species as "experimental populations," either essential or nonessential.) If a red wolf wanders onto private land and attacks a sheep or cow, the owner will not be prosecuted for shooting the wolf.

The U.S. Fish and Wildlife Service has a fund provided by private organizations that will reimburse owners for livestock killed. In the first six months at the Great Smoky National Park, $253 was paid out of the fund when a chicken and a new calf were reported missing and it seemed likely that red wolves were responsible.

With the cooperation of local ranchers, biologists deliberately released one wolf family in a grassy valley not far from cattle pastures, in order to learn whether the wolves would prey on livestock. This wolf family stayed together, hunting in a pack and eating mainly woodchucks, rabbits, and deer. But they also killed some young calves. The wildlife biologists are working with the livestock owner on ways to protect the herd and helped to build a "nursery corral," fenced with extra strands of barbed wire, to keep the young calves safer.

THE RED WOLF'S SUCCESS

By the fall of 1993 the red wolf population was close to 250, with more than 50 in the wild. The return of the red wolf represented the first time a captive-bred North American mammal had become extinct in the wild and had been returned successfully to a native habitat. There is still a long way to go, though, before red wolves are fully reestablished in the wild.

The red wolf program has moved ahead quickly over the years. But other wolf programs have not. For years, there have been plans to reintroduce gray wolves into Yellowstone, and little progress has been made with a Mexican wolf program. There are several reasons why red wolf plans have proceeded but other plans haven't. The native wolf populations in the East had disappeared more than a century ago, and most people living there did not have strong negative feelings against wolves. So when they were carefully informed about the aims and the methods of the recovery program, they were willing to give it a chance. In the West, though, there is a much more active livestock industry, and the wool and cattle growers' associations are very strong. They still remember when wolves killed livestock, and they have been fighting plans to reintroduce these predators.

However, the red wolf's success is helping to pave the way for other wolves, too. The experience of the reintroduction program has demonstrated that wolves and people can exist side by side.

WOLF OR MUTT: A HOWLING CONTROVERSY

In the 1970s, Ronald Nowak and other biologists with the Fish and Wildlife Service studied skulls of red wolves, gray wolves, coyotes, and fossil remains of wild canines that historically lived in the Southeast. They concluded that the red wolf was a separate species. In fact, it was suggested that red wolves existed before gray wolves. A theory was proposed that red wolves probably descended from a canid that evolved in North America.

A million years ago, some of these wolflike animals crossed over to Eurasia. When wolves eventually returned, the scientists speculated, they had evolved into gray wolves, which pushed the red wolves into their now historic range. Fish and Wildlife biologists justified the breeding and reintroduction programs on the basis of this research.

By 1991 the red wolf had become a shining example of the Endangered Species Act in action. Thanks to the red wolf recovery plan, these wolves had been successfully saved from extinction, bred in captivity, and released into the wild.

In June 1991, a new study was published that opened up the whole question again. Two scientists who were experts in wildlife genetics, Robert K. Wayne and Susan M. Jenks of the University of California, examined the genetic material (called DNA) in a part of red wolf cells called mitochondria. They took samples from nearly 100 red wolves, including genetic material from wolf furs that date from the beginning of this century. The researchers could not find a unique genetic pattern that only red wolves share. In every case the genetic material from the red wolf cells matched either coyote or gray wolf DNA.

IS THE RED WOLF A MUTT?

Scientists are not sure how to interpret this information. One explanation might be that red wolves are just hybrids produced when gray wolves mated with coyotes. A second explanation is that red wolves crossbred with coyotes a long time ago, so that they no longer have their own unique "genetic fingerprint."

But if the red wolf is not really a unique species, what is the point of spending all that public money to protect and reintroduce it? Wildlife scientists began a heated argument that seemed to threaten the survival of not only the red wolf but many other endangered plant and animal species as well.

If the red wolf is indeed a hybrid, it is not legally entitled to protection under the Endangered Species Act. In the late 1970s, the Fish and Wildlife Service had decided to deny protection to hybrid plant and animal species in order to preserve the unique traits of closely related species. At that time, no one imagined that decision would be used by opponents of the Endangered Species Act to have animals such as the red wolf taken off the endangered species list.

**Some researchers think the red wolf is actually a cross
between the gray wolf and the coyote, shown here.**

Soon the debate about what makes up a species was making head-
lines. Within weeks of the publication of the study, cattle and sheep
ranchers in Tennessee and North Carolina petitioned the Fish and Wildlife Service to remove the red wolf from the endangered species list. The
request was denied, on the grounds that further study was needed.

The Endangered Species Act

THE Endangered Species Act was passed in 1973 to provide protection for animals and plants that have become endangered or threatened with extinction. By 1993, about 700 American plant and animal species had been placed on the endangered species list. There are enough funds to evaluate only about 50 species a year. But there are thousands of threatened species that have not been evaluated yet. Recovery plans have not been drawn up for many of those listed, and some species have had to be taken off the list because they are already extinct.

TOO HIGH A PRICE?

The hybrid debate is giving new ammunition to the people who want to develop wildlife areas. They have been arguing that industry and jobs in an area are more important than the welfare of plants and animals. Industry representatives say that not only is it impossible to list and protect all the species that scientists claim should be protected, but the price is just too high to pay for so little benefit. (In 1991, $764,000 was spent for the red wolf restoration project, not counting biologists' salaries. The programs for 29 other endangered species cost even more.) But if it could be proved that the red wolf and some other endangered species are really hybrids, the expensive recovery programs for them could be eliminated. New methods like DNA testing could provide the proof.

Biologists point out that life in the wild is hard for the red wolf. They estimate the life expectancy of a free-roaming Carolina red wolf is only three to four years. This is enough time for it to reproduce at least once, so that eventually there will be a self-sustaining population of wild red wolves. But scientists cannot guarantee that if the red wolf is ever reestablished in the wild, it will not mate with coyotes and become endangered again.

Even some scientists believe the red wolf should not be protected. They argue that since it is impossible to protect all the animals and plants threatened with extinction, we should just try to protect "keystone species"—organisms that are necessary to preserve an entire ecosystem. These scientists suggest that since coyotes have already filled the red wolf's ecological niche, money spent for the red wolf should be spent elsewhere. They point out that even if red wolves became extinct, their genes would survive in wolves and coyotes. Other scientists say this controversy points out the need to protect whole ecosystems, not just individual animals within those ecosystems.

IN DEFENSE OF THE RED WOLF

Meanwhile, Robert Wayne says his study was misinterpreted; the results were just preliminary and should not be used as the basis for a major decision like dropping protection for the red wolf. He points out that even if the wolf does turn out to be a hybrid, it might be impossible to reproduce the special conditions that originally created the mixture. Gray wolves and coyotes have crossbred in Minnesota and Canada, for example, and yet red wolves have never lived in those areas.

Perhaps there was once a unique red wolf species, Wayne points out, and it was replaced by a hybrid because of extermination campaigns and human activities that destroyed the wolf's original habitat. "You could make a case," he says, "that, as the last living example of an extinct species, these hybrids are worth saving. They're all we have left of a species that humans killed off."[8]

Researchers are fearful that as genetic testing becomes more common, more endangered species will be called into question. Already other studies have found the Florida panther may have become a hybrid by interbreeding with South American cougars, and a threatened gray wolf in Minnesota and Canada has bred with coyotes.

The Species Debate

SINCE THE 1940s, scientists have generally accepted the "Biological Species Concept," a theory presented by Ernst Mayr. According to the theory, one way to tell a specific species from another is to observe whether or not these organisms mate with each other. Grizzly bears will not mate with black bears, for example. However, the theory does not work with animals such as canids (wolves, coyotes, and domestic dogs), which are all capable of breeding with one another under certain conditions, even though they are recognized as separate species.

In 1991, Ernst Mayr co-authored an article that pointed out that living creatures are constantly evolving. New species may be created when hybrids are formed. To say that hybrids should not be protected could thus interfere with an important natural process.

GENETIC TECHNOLOGY: SAVIOR OR SPOILER?

Genetic technology has become a useful tool for scientists in their quest to help save endangered animals. By using DNA testing, for example, they can determine which animals to breed to maintain the purest genes in a species.

Will new molecular biology techniques help biologists preserve natural diversity, or—as some business interests hope and conservationists fear—will it provide the ammunition to reduce the number of animals and plants protected by the Endangered Species Act?

The Fish and Wildlife Service is developing a new hybrid policy that would consider genetic research results, but would also place heavy emphasis on the natural history of rare organisms. Fish and Wildlife Service biologists say that all over the world, human activities have disrupted habitats and made interbreeding among rare species much more common. The new policy therefore has to be flexible enough to protect even hybrids, when their existence is due to human effects on wildlife. It would allow protection to continue for the red wolf and other species, such as the gray wolf and Florida panther.

Meanwhile, the red wolf continues to make its comeback. Though human activities brought it close to extinction, now humans are helping to save it.

NOTES

1. V. Banks, "The Red Wolf Gets a Second Chance to Live by Its Wits," *Smithsonian*, March 1988, p. 107.

2. Jan DeBlieu, *Meant to Be Wild* (Golden, Colorado: Fulcrum, 1991), p. 31.

3. DeBlieu, p. 34.

4. DeBlieu, p. 44.

5. DeBlieu, p. 43.

6. Vince Magers, "Coming Home: A Journey Back from Near Extinction," *ZOOmin'*, Spring 1989, p. 38.

7. Peter Radetsky, "Back to Nature," *Discover*, July 1993, p. 40.

8. Jan DeBlieu, "Could the Red Wolf Be a Mutt?" *New York Times Magazine*, June 14, 1992, p. 46.

FACTS ABOUT THE RED WOLF

Size	About 41 inches (104 centimeters) long plus a 14-inch (35.5-centimeter) tail and about 25 inches (63.5 centimeters) tall
Weight	40 to 70 pounds (18 to 32 kilograms)
Color	Typically tan or cinnamon-brown, streaked with black; some coats have a gold or reddish tint; some are all gray or black
Food	Small animals, such as raccoons, rabbits, squirrels, muskrats, rats, fish, small deer, and insects and plant material
Reproduction	They mate for life; they breed in February or March of their second or third year; after 63 days a litter of 2 to 6 pups is born
Care for young	The mother leaves pups only to drink; the male brings her food; both parents keep an eye on their young
Range	Southern part of the United States; now restricted to managed wild colonies in North Carolina refuges and breeding centers such as Tacoma, Washington
Population size	About 250 red wolves
Social behavior	Sociable animals that live in family groups of parents, children, and close relatives; they work together as a team to raise the pups, hunt food, and defend each other against enemies
Life span	10 to 15 years or more in captivity; about 6 years in the wild

FURTHER READING

Books

DeBlieu, Jan. *Meant to Be Wild*. Golden, Colorado: Fulcrum, 1991.

Patent, Dorothy Hinshaw. *Gray Wolf–Red Wolf*. New York: Clarion, 1990.

Pamphlets and Newsletters

"Endangered Species: The Red Wolf (*Canis rufus*)," U.S. Fish and Wildlife Service.

Red Wolf Newsletter, Point Defiance Zoo & Aquarium.

Red Wolf Update: Recovery in the Smokies, National Park Service and U.S. Fish and Wildlife Service.

Wolf! magazine.

Wolftracks, Wolf Haven International.

ORGANIZATIONS TO CONTACT

Defenders of Wildlife
1244 Nineteenth Street, NW
Washington, DC 20036
(202) 659-9510

Endangered Species Field Office
U.S. Fish and Wildlife Service
100 Otis Street, Room 224
Asheville, NC 28802

Great Smoky Mountains National Park
Gatlinburg, TN 37738
(615) 436-1207

North American Wolf Foundation, Inc.
98 Essex Street
Ipswich, MA 01938

Point Defiance Zoo & Aquarium
5400 North Pearl Street
Tacoma, WA 98407
(206) 305-1000

The Red Wolf Fund
c/o The Tacoma Zoological Society
5400 North Pearl Street
Tacoma, WA 98407

The Red Wolf Sanctuary
P.O. Box 235
Dillsboro, IN 47018
(812) 667-5303

U.S. Fish and Wildlife Service
Publications Unit
Washington, DC 20240

Wild Canid Survival
  & Research Center
P.O. Box 760
Eureka, MO 63025

Wolf Haven International
3111 Offut Lake Road
Tenino, WA 98589

INDEX

Page numbers in *italics* refer to illustrations.

ABOUT THE AUTHORS

Alvin Silverstein is a
professor of biology at the
City University of New York,
College of Staten Island;
Virginia Silverstein, his wife,
is a translator of Russian scientific literature. Together they
have published nearly 100 books
on science and health topics.

Robert Silverstein joined his
parents' writing team in 1988
and has since co-authored more
than a dozen books with them,
including the Food Power! nutrition
series from The Millbrook Press.